Rhyme and
some Nottinghamshire
Folk tales

by Stan Smith

The Nottinghamshire Heritage Series.
Happy Walking International Ltd.
1998

Happy Walking International Ltd.,
Unit 1,
Molyneux Business Park,
Whitworth Road,
Darley Dale,
Matlock,
Derbyshire
DE4 2HJ
Tel/Fax 01629 - 735911
E-Mail - john.merrill@virgin.net

Printed, bound, marketed and distributed by Happy Walking International Ltd.

Produced by a member of
THE GUILD OF MASTER CRAFTSMEN

First Published - September 1998

ISBN 1 874754

British Library Cataloguing-in-Publication Data. A catalogue record of this book is available from the British Library.

Typeset in AGaramond - bold, italic, and plain 12pt, 14pt and 18pt.

CONTENTS

Thanks...
I wish to record my thanks to my wife Christine Smith who, as always, helped me with proof reading and provides me with the necessary support and encouragement.

My thanks also go to poet Tony Wass - Chairman of the Nottingham Writers' Club - and poet Sue Challand who again were supportive and made valuable suggestions - especially in connection with the verse content of this book

I am happy to dedicate this book to all three.

WEARY, WINDY, MILLER MOSS

Weary, Windy, Miller Moss
Rode upon his old grey hoss
All the way to Mansfield Town
To sell his horse for half a crown.

He found the going hot and tough
And half way there, he'd had enough
But, inns and taverns on the way
Kept him going through the day.

A merry, Windy, Miller Moss
Arrived at Mansfield on his hoss,
But, he arrived too late of course
To get the best price for his horse.

The honest rogues who bought his steed,
Though late the hour, it was agreed,
Would find a younger, sprightly Mare,
To get the Miller here and there.

Sleepy, Windy, Miller Moss,
Travelled homewards on his hoss.
But, truth to tell and strange to say -
That new bought Mare showed him the way!

Weary, Windy, Miller Moss

Miller Moss lived in one of the windmills which once stood in a line at the top of Nottingham's Forest. One day, realising that his faithful old horse was coming to the end of its useful life, he rode it to Mansfield determined to trade it in and then buy a new horse at the town's Horse Fair.

Being a jovial sort, Miller Moss slaked his thirst at a number of inns and taverns on the way to Mansfield and, by the time he got there, was very convivial. Several rogues taking advantage of Miller Moss's incapacity, bought his old horse at a knock down price and, later in the day, disguised the same horse with boot polish and sold it back to him at a vastly inflated price!

By this time, Miller Moss was quite incapable, but, his faithful old horse brought him safely home. One can imagine what Dame Moss, his wife, had to say when she found out what had happened!

THE WHITE LADY

Sophia glides across the lawn
Rues the day that she was born
Sighs a sigh and hangs her head.
Lord Gordon Noel, alas, is dead.

Sophia flits from tree to tree
Her sorrow spans eternity;
Binds her heart in mortal dread.
Lord Gordon Noel, alas, is dead.

Sophia walks beside the lake;
She seeks the path that he would take.
In vain she listens for his tread;
Lord Gordon Noel, alas, is dead.

Sophia's spirit cannot rest
She beats her arms and beats her breast.
And still she wanders - hands outspread.
Lord Gordon Noel, alas, is dead.

The White Lady

The mysterious, White Lady of Newstead Abbey is said to be the ghost of Sophia Hyatt, daughter of a Nottingham Bookseller. This unfortunate lady was an enthusiastic admirer of Lord George Gordon Noel Byron, the famous poet, who lived at Newstead Abbey for a time.

When her parents died, Sophia continued to live in the family home on the Abbey estate, but, completely alone, with a mere pittance to live on. She began to live in the past, on recollections of the days when she had seen Byron walking about the Abbey grounds. Her memories of the poet became such an obsession with her that she spent more and more of her time in contemplation and in retracing the steps of her hero.

In 1824, when Lord Byron died, Sophia was devastated. Some say her mind became unhinged to such an extent that she couldn't rest and began roaming the grounds of the Abbey by day and by night in various stages of disarray. By now Sophia, a deaf, elderly woman, had become a haunted, wraith-like figure. Instead of wearing black, the traditional colour of mourning, she took to wearing white, like a bride on her wedding day.

A little more than a year after Byron's death she travelled to Nottingham by Coach. In Maypole yard, just off Long Row, where the out-of-town coaches set down and picked up fresh passengers, she was knocked down by a Carrier's horse and cart and was killed on the spot.

Sophia Hyatt was buried in Hucknall Churchyard, as near as possible to the vault containing the body of her beloved Byron. But, it is said, even in death she couldn't rest. Some say that, even to this day, the wraith-like figure of the White Lady can be seen searching the grounds of Newstead Abbey!

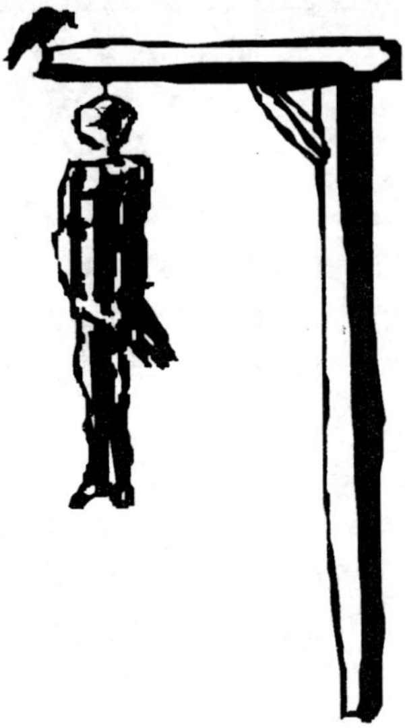

HUSH MY BABIES

Hush my babies, don't you cry,
See the horseman riding by.
See he wears the Royal Ring
Bringing Pardon from the King.

Hush my babies, wait and see,
Soon your daddy will be free,
Free to leave this dreadful place,
Free to share our fond embrace

Hush my babies, don't despair
See the crowd and hear them cheer.
See your daddy, see the rope,
See the Pardon, cling to hope.

Cry my babies, cry for me.
It came too late to set him free!

Hush My Babies

The Public Gallows stood for centuries on Gallows Hill, outside the walls of Old Nottingham town, on an elevated site, a little distance from the "Nag's Head" tavern on Mansfield Road. It is said that many a poor wretch slaked his thirst at this pub before completing his journey which ended with an appointment with the Public Hangman.

In the days when a public execution was an excuse for a holiday and created as much excitement as a modern day Cup Final, taproom customers at the "Nag's Head" got a grandstand view of the proceedings and could watch as the little procession emerged onto Mansfield Road after winding its way from the Shire Hall on High Pavement, or from the Town Hall at Weekday Cross, by way of Bridlesmith Gate, High Street, and Clumber Street.

As the cart drew nearer, forcing its way through the crowds clustered on both sides of the road, it would, as custom dictated, stop so that the condemned man could have a last drink at the tavern before mounting the scaffold. As the cup was carried to the prisoner's lips, the crowd would laugh and jeer by turn, unless it was a personable young man who made the hearts of the ladies flutter because he was so handsome.

Not every condemned man or woman stopped at the tavern, however, for the customary last tankard of ale and there were a few who wanted to get the execution over and done with, not wishing to prolong the agony. Indeed, it is said, that one condemned prisoner actually refused to take a last drink at the tavern and his reprieve arrived just five minutes after he had been turned off the cart! If only he had accepted the permitted last drink, he might well have lived to see his grandchildren. Hush my babies, don't you cry....

CHEESES ABOUND

Send for the Soldiers
Send for the Mayor
We can't sell our cheeses
At Nottingham Fair.

Send for the Farmer
Send for his wife
Without buying cheeses
What good is a knife?

Send for the Sexton
Send for his mate
They're rolling our cheeses
Down old Wheeler Gate

Send for the Parson
Send for the Quack
His Worship the Mayor
Lies flat on his back

Cheeses Abound

Nottingham Goose Fair, which for many years was also a Cheese Fair, is usually a time of great happiness with everyone in holiday mood. However, a disturbance in 1766 turned everything sour!

Farmers in from the Countryside were asking thirty shillings for a hundred-weight of Cheese. Prospective buyers were so exasperated by such blatant overcharging that tempers soon flared and violence broke out. Stalls were overturned and cheeses were spoiled or sent rolling down Peck Lane and Wheeler Gate. His Worship the Mayor, Rob Swann, whilst attempting to restore calm, was himself bowled over in the Market Place by a particularly large cheese.

The Fifteenth Dragoon of Soldiers were hurriedly sent for by the Magistrates and they quelled the disturbance with excessive violence, breaking many heads and shedding much blood. Amazingly there was only one death - that of William Eggleston of Car Colston who was shot on the spot by a Dragoon whilst guarding his cheeses.

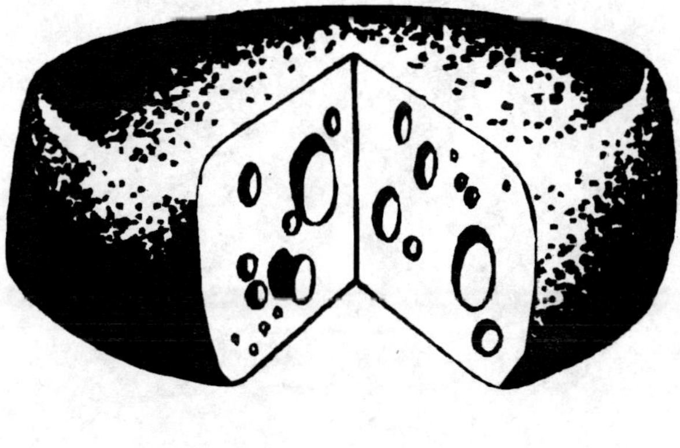

ARABELLA

Arabella walks the floor,
Even though she is no more.
She wrings her hands
And sighs her sighs
She treads her cell
And cries her cries.
Her Royal Blood has brought her down
But, not for want of England's crown!

Elizabeth the First.

Arabella

In 1574, in the chapel of Rufford Abbey, Bess of Hardwick's daughter, Elizabeth Cavendish, married Charles Stuart, Earl of Lennox - the Grandson of Queen Margaret of Scotland. Within a year Lady Arabella Stuart, the only child of the marriage, was born, but, she was orphaned by the time she was 6 - both parents dying in their twenties. Her portrait hung in the drawing room at Rufford Abbey until the contents of the house were sold off in 1938.

Lady Arabella, one of the saddest figures in history was, through her father, the great great granddaughter of King Henry VII of England and next in line to the crown after James I. She was at the centre of plots to put her on the throne in place of her cousin, Elizabeth I, and although innocent, was arrested and placed in prison. On the Queen's death she was again the centre of another plot, but, this time it was intended that she should replace her cousin, James I, the new King! The real ringleaders were said to be Sir Walter Raleigh, Lord Cobham, Lord Grey and the Earl of Northumberland who faced trial for treason. The King was furious with his cousin and imprisoned her at Barnet, from where she later escaped with the help of William Markham of Ollerton.

Seven years later, aged 35, Arabella made an indiscreet marriage with William Seymour, a descendent of the Tudors, a man thirteen years her junior. The King, feeling threatened by strengthening claims to the throne, arrested Seymour, consigned him to the Tower and banished Arabella to Durham in the far North. There, with the aid of friends, she managed to escape disguised as a man and boarded a French ship waiting in the Thames. Her husband, who had also escaped, followed in another ship. Unfortunately for them, a violent sea storm kept them apart and the unfortunate Lady Arabella was captured off Calais and brought back to England. Her husband, whom she was never to see again, landed safely in Ostend..

Cast into the Tower, Lady Arabella, guiltless of any crime, was imprisoned for four years. First her health deteriorated and then her sanity. She died in 1615, aged 40, a broken woman. After her death, her husband returned to England, fought as a Royalist in the Civil Wars and was rewarded with the Dukedom of Somerset by a grateful King Charles II.

Lady Arabella Stuart lies in Westminster Abbey within the tomb of her aunt, Mary Queen of Scots, but, her restless ghost is still said to walk the grounds of Rufford Abbey.

SANDMAN

The Sandman's coming
You sleepy head.
The Sandman's coming
It's time for bed.

Sandman

On Peel Street, just a stone's throw from the City Centre in Nottingham is an ordinary green door, which appears to be the entrance to a war time air raid shelter. Beyond the door is a long flight of stone steps and the privileged few can still be taken on a torchlit tour of the Sandstone Caves of Old Nottingham.

The largest of all the caverns was the work of one man - James Rouse who excavated sand for more than thirty years.

For hundreds of years these caves were the natural working environment of a group of second class townsmen known as Sandmen.

Deep below ground the dreadful damp and cramped conditions of the Sandmen can still be experienced and it is humbling to think that men lived, worked and died in these dreadful surroundings. But, it was all in a day's work for the men who dug the sand so that Nottingham housewives could clean their floors and kitchen utensils.

Few of the old diggers lived to a ripe old age and they often became totally blind from an early age because of a lifetime spent below ground in almost total darkness.

The Sandmen eventually became deformed with rheumatism and arthritis through the damp atmosphere in the caves and most died from a form of tuberculosis aggravated by breathing in fine particles of sand.

It was a very high price to pay for sand which sold on the street at just four pence for a hundred weight sack!

WISE MEN

Lor', Bless you sir, we grew this hedge
To keep our Cuckoo in,
But, Bless me sir, not tall enough
To make it always Spring.

On Summer nights we rake our pond
To float our Cheeses free
And roll them down to Nottingham
To spare our aching knee.

On Autumn days our village sage,
To save his sorry back,
Rides with the load around his neck
Instead of on its back.

But best of all, on Winter nights,
We sup our ale with glee
For good King John has passed us by
And left our village free.

Wise Men

Many are the tales of the Wise Men of Gotham, a village a few miles south of Nottingham. But, the village simpletons knew what they were doing and even fooled King John, himself - and his advisers!

In the early 1200s, it became known that King John was looking for somewhere to build a hunting lodge within riding distance of Nottingham Castle and he was particularly interested in the Gotham area, sending his Courtiers over in advance to spy out the land.

Not wishing to be saddled with the expense of maintaining the King and all his Courtiers, especially as neighbours, the villagers devised a clever plan. Whenever the King's men were around they played the fool to perfection.

A group of locals was found planting thorn bushes around a wood and when asked why they replied that they were caging a cuckoo in the wood so that it would sing for them all year long and it would always be Spring in Gotham.

They rolled cheeses downhill to nearby Nottingham Market in order to save themselves the journey, set fire to the village forge to destroy a wasps nest; unsuccessfully tried to drown eels in water and raked the reflection of the moon from the surface of the village pond because they were convinced it was cheese!

The King's men scratched their heads in amazement at the madness around them, specially when they saw the local miller riding his horse with bags of wheat tied around his own neck - to save his horse from carrying the weight!

When they reported back to King John he hurriedly looked elsewhere to build his Hunting Lodge, convinced that the wise men of Gotham were all fools. But locals have a well known saying "More fools pass through Gotham than stay there!"

ROBIN -THE BUTCHER

Bold Robin met a Butcher
On his way to town
"Pray, sell to me your meat" he said
"And sell to me your gown"

"Your horse and cart, if they're for sale"
I'll gladly also buy.
I'm on my way to Nottingham
I'll be there by and by."

At Nottingham bold Robin
Set up his Market stall
He sold his meat at half the price
To each and one and all.

Other butchers all around,
They ranted and they muttered:
"The varlet with his horse and cart
He must be stopped", they spluttered.

The Sheriff and his men rode up
Intrigued by all the rattle
And made a deal with Robin Hood
To buy up all his cattle.

"My herd is in the deep Greenwood"
Quoth Robin to the buyer
You, alone, must follow me
For the best meat in the Shire."

The wily Sheriff slyly smiled -
His luck was in egad!
To sell those beast at such a price
The knave was clearly mad.

All day and half the night,
The Butcher led the way
Until a wand'ring herd of deer
They came across at play.

"Here's my herd, good Sheriff"
Laughed bold Sir Robin Hood
And from beneath his apron
Took a horn to blast the Wood.

Forest men in Lincoln green
Came by from far and wide.
And how they laughed to see
The Sheriff mortified.

They took from him, his purse of gold
And made him dance and rave.
They made the Sheriff rue the day
He bargained with a knave.

Robin - the Butcher

Robin Hood is a legendary English Outlaw who is thought to have lived in the reign of Richard I. According to tradition, he lived in Sherwood Forest and robbed the rich to give to the poor, surrounding himself with a merry band of outlaws who acknowledged him as their leader.

The stories of Robin are legion, but, this one tells of the time when he met a butcher who was setting off to sell his meat at Nottingham Market. The butcher was not keen to travel so far, but, he had to sell his meat to make a living. Robin persuaded the butcher to sell him his stock of meat and his horse and cart. They then exchanged clothing.

In Nottingham, Robin almost caused a riot among the other butchers, who considered they were being ruined because the stranger was practically giving his meat away.

They complained to the Sheriff of Nottingham who was responsible for law and order in town, and he, suspecting that the butcher was simple in the head, decided that he would profit at the expense of this stranger. He persuaded Robin to sell him all the cattle he owned at a ridiculous sum - a scheme to which Robin happily agreed.

That evening, the Sheriff on horseback, accompanied Robin and his horse and cart back to Sherwood Forest to transact the deal. When they were in the thick of the Forest, Robin showed him a herd of deer. The Sheriff was angry, but, this turned to amazement when Robin produced a horn from under his apron. Three short blasts summoned his Merry Men from all directions.

The men discovered the gold that the Sheriff was carrying and Robin confiscated it all saying : "This will pay for the beasts as we agreed. Now I can return your coins to the poor people you robbed in the first place!"

The Sheriff was very angry at this deceit, but, as Robin said "You were happy enough to swindle a poor country butcher when it suited you. Now the boot is on the other foot". They then blindfolded the Sheriff and turned him loose to return to Nottingham vowing vengeance on Robin and his Merry Men.

THE CAP'N

Where the white of the ground
Meets the white of the sky,
There's no place on earth
So bleak to the eye,
Yet the Cap'n just sits there
As still as can be,
Erect at his table
Marooned by the sea..

The Cap'n

In the summer of 1553, some Russian fishermen discovered a ship floating at anchor at the mouth of the River Arzina on the coast of Lapland. On stepping aboard, they discovered that every single member of the 63-men crew lay dead, sprawling where they had fallen! They had frozen to death the previous winter!

The Captain sat bolt upright in his chair, at a table in his cabin with the ship's log in front of him. His hand rested on a parchment containing his last will and testament - written before death overtook him.

The Captain was Sir Hugh Willoughby of Broxtowe Hall, Nottingham - the son of Sir Henry Willoughby of Wollaton and his third wife Ellen. Sir Hugh, who had led an eventful life, had been a brilliant soldier - having distinguished himself in the Scottish Wars. He turned to the sea, however, when his Patron, the Duke of Somerset, lost Royal favour and was executed.

Sir Hugh was given command of the ship "Bon Esperanza" and with two other vessels, set off to find the north east passage to China by sailing north. In a violent storm off the Lofoten Islands, Sir Hugh lost touch with one of the ships and the remaining two sought anchorage off the coast of Lapland. Finding good anchorage and having sufficient food and warm clothing, the Captain decided to overwinter before resuming his journey in the Spring.

The weather was very savage and inhospitable and the crew, not having enough fuel to keep them warm and sufficient of the right food to nourish them, all perished from the cold or from scurvy - or so it was always thought!

However, a few years ago, a learned paper in the Geographical Journal advanced the theory that the crew actually died of carbon monoxide poisoning. It is now believed that on a bitter, cold winter's day, the crew battened down the hatches and burned sea coal for warmth. Concentrations of gas built up without warning in the unventilated space causing unconsciousness. The men died where they lay!

THE COBBLER'S SONG

Jamie Lee so small and brown
Had a shop in Southwell town.
His shop he stocked with shoes so neat
That they would grace the fairest feet.

From dawn 'til dusk he stitched together
Boots and shoes of finest leather.
He sang and sewed the whole day long
And as he worked he sang this song:

"Buy my shoes. Oh, buy, pray do.
I have made them just for you.
I have made them good and fair,
You'll never buy a better pair!'

People came from out of town,
To buy such boots of great renown.
The gentry came from far and wide
As did the farmer, groom and bride.

The Greatest, with no time to loose,
Also came to buy some shoes
But standing there with hands on hip,
The cobbler's song died on his lip.

Before him, as his dream foretold,
There stood a man who carried gold.
Who carrying silk upon his feet
Was touched by death, and faced defeat.

Glory to the Lord, our God, Amen.
The Cobbler never sang his song again.

It was the custom of King Charles I to wander around the towns he visited and so it was, at the time of the English Civil War in 1645, at Southwell in Nottinghamshire, that he went into the shop of a cobbler and shoemaker named James Lee. Delighted at not being recognised, the King asked to be measured for a pair of shoes.

As soon as James Lee took the King's foot into his hand, he became very distressed, vividly recalling a bad dream from the night before. When the cobbler refused to continue to measure his feet, the King demanded to know what the matter was.

Dreadfully upset, James Lee told the King that he had dreamed about a foot such as this and it was foretold that the owner of such a foot would bring bad luck to everyone he met and that this man would eventually come to a terrible end. The King, remembering all the set backs that had occurred to him recently, gloomily left the shop without his new shoes.

News of the King's presence at Southwell, reached Colonel Hutchinson in Nottingham Castle and he sent a troop of two hundred horse to attempt his capture. But, they arrived too late, because the King had gone.

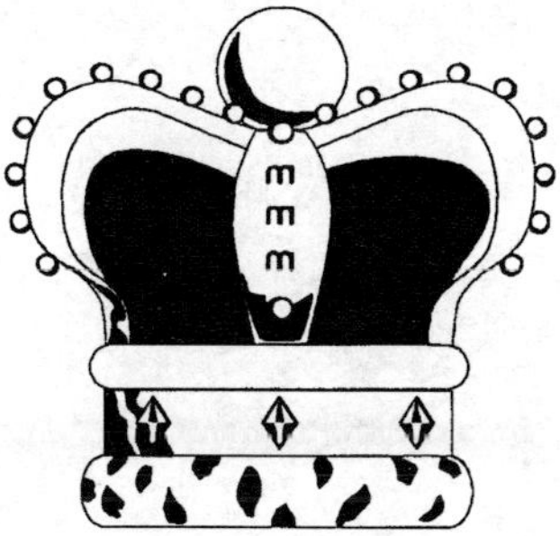

GOOSEY GANDER

Goosey Gander follow me
Along the King's Highway.
See the Parson in his hat
On his way to pray.

Goosey Gander follow me
Over hill and dale.
See the Squire on his horse;
See him quaff his ale.

Goosey Gander follow me
On to Nottingham.
See the Soldier in his coat;
See him with his gun.

Goosey Gander follow me
To the Market cross.
See the tailor and his wife;
See them stroll across.

Goosey Gander we must part
Now our journey's done.
See the pennies in my hand;
See me turn and run.

Goosey Gander

Nottingham is justly famous for its Goose Fair which has been held almost continuously for more than 700 years. Nowadays it is a pleasure fair with roundabouts, rides, side shows, candy floss and all the fun of the fair. But, in its early days, it was a fair, or market, for selling Geese which were fattened up all through the year ready for the Michaelmas Feast of St Michael on September 29th. Most families cooked and ate goose then, just as we roast turkey at Christmastime nowadays.

When the Geese were ready for Market, their feet were tarred for the long walk ahead and they were driven by younger members of the family all the way to Nottingham town which was often many miles away.

At the Fair, the youngsters made the best bargain they could for the Geese, bought whatever things the family needed and then walked all the way home with whatever pennies were left.

REMEMBER ME

Baker, Baker, bake me bread,
Thank the Lord that I'm not dead
Thank my God and feed His poor
Rejoice with me for evermore.

Baker, Baker, warm the bowl,
Pray our God shall keep us whole.
Save us from the fire and sword
That we may live to praise the Lord.

Baker, Baker, prove your worth
Feed the hungry here on earth.
Three times I tossed, three times I turned
Three times I dreamt my house had burned.

Baker, Baker, knead your dough,
Empty is the street below.
Hurry daughter, hurry wife
Come my son and save your life.

Baker, Baker, swell your yeast
Receive my treasure from the priest.
In days to come when men are free
With bread and prayers, remember me.

Remember Me

In Newark, near Nottingham, the custom was revived of giving special loaves of bread to the poor to celebrate a miracle which occurred during the English Civil War in 1643. This miracle, concerning a man named Hercules Clay, took place during the siege of Newark by Cromwell's soldiers.

Hercules had a house in the Market Place and one night he dreamed the same dream over and over again. He was convinced that his house would catch fire and he could not rest until he had woken his family, made them dress and hurried them out of the house in the middle of the night. They thought that he was mad and grumbled as they tumbled out onto the street at three o'clock in the morning!

Less than a quarter of an hour later, a bombardment scored a direct hit on Hercules's house and it was burned to the ground. Sadly the Parliamentarians, were aiming at the Governor's house on the far side of the Market Place, but their aim was wide of the mark and it was Hercules Clay's house that was destroyed.

So that the whole town would know of his miraculous escape, Hercules made an endowment to the Parish church of £200, some of which was to be used to buy bread for the poor on the anniversary of his salvation. Two years later Alderman Hercules Clay, one time Mayor of Newark, was dead. He is commemorated by a monument in the south chancel aisle of the Parish Church.

TWO KINDS OF CHRISTMAS

White is the colour of the old man's beard
Grey is the colour of his sack
Red is the colour of his fur lined boots
But, crooked is the old man's back

White is the colour of a dolly's dress
Grey are the soldiers made from tin
Red is the colour of the fire in the grate
But frozen are the poor man's kin.

White is the colour of snow underfoot
Grey is the colour of the sky
Red is the colour of a rich man's wine
But hunger makes a brave man cry.

Two Kinds of Christmas

"The rich man in his castle the poor man at his gate" so goes the verse illustrating the two worlds of the "haves" and the "have nots". The contrasts between the rich and poor of Victorian England was a favourite theme of Charles Dickens and in most generations there continues to be a divide between the comfortably off and the people who live in cardboard city.

In Dickens day, the only alternative to living on the streets for the very poor was the workhouse and a family would have to be very desperate indeed to enter such a dismal place - preferring to beg and suffer in any kind of slum. Even so, the workhouse at Southwell was held to be the very best of its kind and was the model used for the Poor Law Amendment Act of 1834. But, life was still grim. Men were separated from wives and children. They wore a degrading uniform and lived on a diet of potatoes, vegetables and thin porridge gruel.

At Southwell, as elsewhere, able bodied men had to work hard for their meagre allowance of food, growing potatoes and vegetables in the workhouse grounds, picking oakum and breaking stones. They also crushed bones, hard, repulsive work which was mercifully stopped following the Andover Scandal where starving men were found eating gristle and marrow from the bones.

Children fared no better. They were treated as young adults and had to work hard to survive - or take to the streets to beg borrow and steal. They had no toys and dollies like the richer children. and Christmas to them was just another hungry day. Santa never called and a crust of bread was the nearest they would ever get to plum pudding.

Workhouses were abolished in 1930.

SONG O' THE GENERAL

I marched my men across the Square.
I marched my soldiers everywhere.
I drilled them left; I drilled them right.
I drilled them hard from morn 'til night.

I marched them up; I marched them down.
I marched my soldiers through the town.
From New Exchange to Weekday Cross,
From Shire Hall to Flying Hoss.

I marched them in, I marched them out
I marched my soldiers round about
From yard to court; from street to pen,
Behind the Mayor and all his men.

Song of the General

Ben Mayo, otherwise "The Old General", was a well known eccentric, who spent the whole of his life in one Nottingham workhouse or another. He was born in St Peter's Work House, Broad Marsh in 1778 and died in St Mary's Workhouse, Mansfield Road, 64 years later. The ringleader of the boys of the town, he received his nick name from an early age.

Ben was not a very imposing figure with his shuffling gait, rounded shoulders and high forehead topped with a thinning, cropped, "institutional" haircut. In his early years he wore a drab, grey workhouse uniform, but, later his friend, Mr Hudson, gave him a scarlet coat with military epaulettes. In all weathers his shirt remained obstinately unfastened, revealing a large expanse of copper coloured chest.

He was in his element with the boys of the town, taking great pleasure in drilling them like soldiers in the Market Square. For this and other antics he became a well known, local figure.

Ben also had a wicked sense of fun, typically shown when selling broadsheets in the streets. "Read all about it!" he would shout. "One penny for the DUKE OF YORK'S latest speech!" After selling out completely he would make himself scarce, but, if one of his disgruntled customers tackled him about the blank sheets he would explain with a cheeky grin: "Well, what did you expect. The Duke said nowt."

Every year, in September, the Mayor and Corporation "beat the bounds" by walking around Nottingham's boundary and then, a few days later, toured the town looking for nuisances and obstructions, such as the keeping of pigs in yards or piling dung in the streets. Notes would be taken of actions needed. Following behind would come the Old General with his army of schoolboys "liberated" from their lessons. But, ***they*** didn't take notes! They took immediate action - bearing away the troublesome shoe scraper, or flattening the offending dung heap!

DEAD OF NIGHT

The church bell clangs in the dead of night
As the world and his wife lie sleeping
For the inky black river has climbed out of bed
To come twisting and sliding and creeping.

Night-shirted men and maids in their white shifts
From their sleep by the bell are awaken
But the light of a candle throws only shadows
To frighten the lost and forsaken.

Men in their night-caps watch from their window
As old Father Trent flows under the door;
All through the village, down to the school house
Round by the church and up through the floor.

Loud in the night comes the call of the church bell
Loud is the clangour and din
But stout-hearted men trapped high in their chambers
Lie helpless and hopeless within.

Mothers with children pray for deliverance
From torment that comes with the night
And high in the nursery soft words of comfort
Are tempered with prayers for respite.

Respite from the darkness, respite from the water
An end to the filth and the mud.
Relief from the wearisome clang of the church bell
An end to the terror and flood.

Dead of Night

One terrible night, in 1875, the River Trent overflowed its banks and flooded the little village of Girton, near Besthorpe, in Nottinghamshire. All the villagers were trapped in their bedrooms - high above the street and the rising water.

Then, in the dead of night, the church bell began to ring - tolling a dreadful warning through the darkness. The village people, marooned in their homes and surrounded by floodwater, could do nothing but pray!

Days went by before the floods subsided and only then could the terrified villagers creep from their houses to visit the church. There, fearfully pushing open the creaking wooden door, they wondered what they would find.

The last thing on earth they expected to find was cows. Cows!

Cows from the fields, sheltering from flood water, had found their way into the church, which was on dry, higher ground. For the last few days, whilst the terrified villagers had prayed for deliverance, the cows had happily munched on the bell rope made of straw!

Nottinghamshire Heritage Series -

BELL TALES *by Stan Smith*
SOME NOTTINGHAMSHIRE PUB STORIES *by Stan Smith*
Rhyme and Reason - *some Nottinghamshire Folk Tales by Stan Smith*

FOR CONSPICUOUS GALLANTRY - Local V.C. Holders - *by N. McCrery*

HISTORY OF SUTTON IN ASHFIELD - *facsimile of 1907 edition*

LORD BYRON *" Mad, bad and dangerous to know."- by E. Eisenberg*

NOTTINGHAMSHIRE STREET TO STREET GUIDE .

THE OLD NORTH ROAD *by Joan Board*
A TO Z OF PILGRIM COUNTRY *by Joan Board*

WOLLATON HALL *by Elizabeth May*
Wollaton as a family home and Natural History Museum

COUNTRY POETRY *by Leslie Williamson*
Nottingham Verse - *"The Soul of the City" by Alsion Davies*

MARY & WILLIAM - a north Midland couple *by Joy Dunicliff*

BASFORD - Village to Suburb *by A.S.Bowley*

For a free catalog of titles - more than 300 - please write to -

Happy Walking International Ltd.,
Unit 1, Molyneux Business Park,
Whitworth Road, Darley Dale,
Derbyshire. DE4 2HJ

Ghosts & Legends Series -

DERBYSHIRE & THE PEAK DISTRICT -

DERBYSHIRE GHOSTS by Wayne Anthony Boylan . ISBN 0 946404 67 4

STRANGE TALES OF THE PEAK by Richard Lichfield. ISBN.0 946404

THE ADVENTURES OF A BAKEWELL GOBLIN by Ben Andrews.

PEAK DISTRICT MONSTERS by Alan Smith.

LEGENDS OF DERBYSHIRE by John N. Merrill

DERBYSHIRE FOLKLORE by John N. Merrill

CUSTOMS OF DERBYSHIRE & THE PEAK DISTRICT by John N. Merrill

NOTTINGHAMSHIRE -

GHOST HUNTING AROUND NOTTINGHAMSHIRE by Rosemary Robb . ISBN 0 946404

GHOSTS & LEGENDS OF NEWARK by Rosemary Robb. ISBN 0 946404

THE RESTLESS SPIRIT - more ghosts and legends - by Rosemary Robb

THE GHOSTS OF WOLLATON HALL by Keith Taylor. 1SBN 0 946404

HAUNTED NOTTINGHAMSHIRE - Vol 1 - by Len Moakes . ISBN 0 946404 31 3

HAUNTED NOTTINGHAMSHIRE - Vol 2 - by Len Moakes . ISBN 0 946404 72 0

NOTTINGHAMSHIRE RAILWAY GHOSTS by John R. Smalley . ISBN 0 946404

OTHER BOOKS FROM Happy Walking International Ltd.,

CIRCULAR WALK GUIDES -

SHORT CIRCULAR WALKS IN THE PEAK DISTRICT - Vol. 1,2 and 3
CIRCULAR WALKS IN WESTERN PEAKLAND
SHORT CIRCULAR WALKS IN THE STAFFORDSHIRE MOORLANDS
SHORT CIRCULAR WALKS - TOWNS & VILLAGES OF THE PEAK DISTRICT
SHORT CIRCULAR WALKS AROUND MATLOCK
SHORT CIRCULAR WALKS IN "PEAK PRACTICE COUNTRY."
SHORT CIRCULAR WALKS IN THE DUKERIES
SHORT CIRCULAR WALKS IN SOUTH YORKSHIRE
SHORT CIRCULAR WALKS IN SOUTH DERBYSHIRE
SHORT CIRCULAR WALKS AROUND BUXTON
SHORT CIRCULAR WALKS AROUND WIRKSWORTH
SHORT CIRCULAR WALKS IN THE HOPE VALLEY
40 SHORT CIRCULAR WALKS IN THE PEAK DISTRICT
CIRCULAR WALKS ON KINDER & BLEAKLOW
SHORT CIRCULAR WALKS IN SOUTH NOTTINGHAMSHIRE
SHIRT CIRCULAR WALKS IN CHESHIRE
SHORT CIRCULAR WALKS IN WEST YORKSHIRE
WHITE PEAK DISTRICT AIRCRAFT WRECKS
CIRCULAR WALKS IN THE DERBYSHIRE DALES
SHORT CIRCULAR WALKS FROM BAKEWELL
SHORT CIRCULAR WALKS IN LATHKILL DALE
CIRCULAR WALKS IN THE WHITE PEAK
SHORT CIRCULAR WALKS IN EAST DEVON
SHORT CIRCULAR WALKS AROUND HARROGATE
SHORT CIRCULAR WALKS IN CHARNWOOD FOREST
SHORT CIRCULAR WALKS AROUND CHESTERFIELD
SHORT CIRCULAR WALKS IN THE YORKS DALES - Vol 1 - Southern area.
SHORT CIRCULAR WALKS IN THE AMBER VALLEY (Derbyshire)
SHORT CIRCULAR WALKS IN THE LAKE DISTRICT
SHORT CIRCULAR WALKS IN THE NORTH YORKSHIRE MOORS
SHORT CIRCULAR WALKS IN EAST STAFFORDSHIRE
DRIVING TO WALK - 16 Short Circular walks south of London by Dr. Simon Archer Vol 1 and 2
LONG CIRCULAR WALKS IN THE PEAK DISTRICT - Vol.1,2 and 3.
WHITE PEAK AIRCRAFT WRECK WALKS
LONG CIRCULAR WALKS IN THE STAFFORDSHIRE MOORLANDS
LONG CIRCULAR WALKS IN CHESHIRE
WALKING THE TISSINGTON TRAIL
WALKING THE HIGH PEAK TRAIL
WALKING THE MONSAL TRAIL & OTHER DERBYSHIRE TRAILS
40 WALKS WITH THE SHERWOOD FORESTER by Doug Harvey

CANAL WALKS -

VOL 1 - DERBYSHIRE & NOTTINGHAMSHIRE
VOL 2 - CHESHIRE & STAFFORDSHIRE
VOL 3 - STAFFORDSHIRE
VOL 4 - THE CHESHIRE RING
VOL 5 - LINCOLNSHIRE & NOTTINGHAMSHIRE
VOL 6 - SOUTH YORKSHIRE
VOL 7 - THE TRENT & MERSEY CANAL
VOL 8 - WALKING THE DERBY CANAL RING

JOHN MERRILL DAY CHALLENGE WALKS -

WHITE PEAK CHALLENGE WALK
DARK PEAK CHALLENGE WALK
PEAK DISTRICT END TO END WALKS
STAFFORDSHIRE MOORLANDS CHALLENGE WALK

WHILE IN THE PEAK DISTRICT VISIT JOHN MERRILL'S HAPPY WALKING SHOP, LATHKILL DALE CRAFT CENTRE, OVER HADDON, NR. BAKEWELL

For a full list of titles - more than 300 - write for a free catalog to-

Happy Walking
International Ltd.,
Unit 1,
Molyneux Business Park,
Whitworth Road,
Darley Dale,
Matlock,
Derbyshire.
DE4 2HJ

PROF. DECLAN KENNEDY
GINSTERWEG 4
D-31595 STEYERBERG
TEL.: +49 5764 2158
KENNEDY@DECLAN.DE

Translated: Elisa Graf, Steyerberg, 2020
Editor + Lay-out + Cover Design: Declan Kennedy
and Jörn Strauss, Steyerberg
Image credit: Kennedy Archive
ISBN: (see back cover)
Production: *epubli* - a Service of *neopubli*, Berlin